50 Avocado Dishes

By: Kelly Johnson

Table of Contents

- Avocado Toast
- Avocado Smoothie
- Guacamole
- Avocado Salad
- Avocado and Egg Breakfast Bowl
- Avocado Salsa
- Avocado Hummus
- Avocado Ice Cream
- Avocado and Tomato Salad
- Avocado Pasta
- Avocado and Cucumber Rolls
- Avocado Deviled Eggs
- Avocado Brownies
- Avocado Chicken Salad
- Avocado and Black Bean Tacos
- Avocado Sushi Rolls
- Avocado and Mango Salad
- Avocado and Sweet Potato Toast
- Avocado Fries
- Avocado and Shrimp Salad
- Avocado and Feta Toast
- Avocado Chocolate Mousse
- Avocado and Chickpea Salad
- Avocado Pizza
- Avocado and Spinach Smoothie
- Avocado Egg Salad
- Grilled Avocado
- Avocado and Kale Salad
- Avocado and Corn Salad
- Avocado and Lentil Bowl
- Avocado and Tuna Salad
- Avocado and Beet Salad
- Avocado and Edamame Dip
- Avocado and Roasted Vegetable Sandwich
- Avocado and Bacon Salad

- Avocado and Crab Salad
- Avocado and Pesto Pasta
- Avocado and Watermelon Salad
- Avocado and Quinoa Salad
- Avocado and Pineapple Salsa
- Avocado and Cucumber Soup
- Avocado and Zucchini Noodles
- Avocado and Pea Smash
- Avocado and Radish Salad
- Avocado and Smoked Salmon Salad
- Avocado and Eggplant Spread
- Avocado and Roasted Pepper Salad
- Avocado and Arugula Salad
- Avocado and Lime Sorbet
- Avocado and Roasted Chickpea Bowl

Avocado Toast

Ingredients:

- 2 slices of whole grain bread
- 1 ripe avocado
- Salt and pepper to taste
- Optional toppings: cherry tomatoes, poached egg, radish slices, chili flakes

Instructions:

1. Toast the bread slices to your preference.
2. Mash the avocado in a bowl and season with salt and pepper.
3. Spread the avocado mixture over the toasted bread.
4. Add your favorite toppings and serve.

Avocado Smoothie

Ingredients:

- 1 ripe avocado
- 1 banana
- 1 cup almond milk (or any milk of choice)
- 1 tablespoon honey or maple syrup
- Ice cubes (optional)

Instructions:

1. Scoop out the avocado flesh and place it in a blender.
2. Add the banana, almond milk, honey, and ice cubes.
3. Blend until smooth and creamy.
4. Serve chilled.

Guacamole

Ingredients:

- 2 ripe avocados
- 1 lime, juiced
- 1/4 cup diced onion
- 2 tablespoons chopped fresh cilantro
- 1 garlic clove, minced
- 1 jalapeño, finely chopped (optional)
- Salt and pepper to taste

Instructions:

1. Mash the avocados in a bowl with a fork.
2. Stir in lime juice, onion, cilantro, garlic, and jalapeño.
3. Season with salt and pepper.
4. Serve with tortilla chips or as a side dish.

Avocado Salad

Ingredients:

- 2 ripe avocados, sliced
- 1 cucumber, sliced
- 1 cup cherry tomatoes, halved
- 1/4 red onion, thinly sliced
- 2 tablespoons olive oil
- 1 tablespoon lemon juice
- Salt and pepper to taste

Instructions:

1. In a bowl, combine avocado, cucumber, cherry tomatoes, and red onion.
2. Drizzle with olive oil and lemon juice.
3. Season with salt and pepper.
4. Toss gently and serve.

Avocado and Egg Breakfast Bowl

Ingredients:

- 1 ripe avocado
- 2 eggs, poached or fried
- 1 cup cooked quinoa or rice
- 1/2 cup cherry tomatoes, halved
- 1 tablespoon olive oil
- Salt and pepper to taste

Instructions:

1. Slice the avocado and arrange it in a bowl with cooked quinoa or rice.
2. Add the cherry tomatoes and poached or fried eggs.
3. Drizzle with olive oil and season with salt and pepper.
4. Serve immediately.

Avocado Salsa

Ingredients:

- 2 ripe avocados, diced
- 1 cup diced tomatoes
- 1/2 cup diced red onion
- 1 jalapeño, finely chopped
- 1/4 cup chopped fresh cilantro
- 1 lime, juiced
- Salt and pepper to taste

Instructions:

1. In a bowl, combine avocado, tomatoes, red onion, jalapeño, and cilantro.
2. Drizzle with lime juice and season with salt and pepper.
3. Toss gently and serve as a dip or topping.

Avocado Hummus

Ingredients:

- 1 ripe avocado
- 1 can (15 oz) chickpeas, rinsed and drained
- 2 tablespoons tahini
- 2 garlic cloves
- 1 lemon, juiced
- 1/4 cup olive oil
- Salt and pepper to taste

Instructions:

1. In a food processor, blend chickpeas, tahini, garlic, and lemon juice until smooth.
2. Add avocado and blend until creamy.
3. Drizzle in olive oil while blending and season with salt and pepper.
4. Serve with pita bread or veggies.

Avocado Ice Cream

Ingredients:

- 2 ripe avocados
- 1 cup heavy cream
- 1/2 cup sweetened condensed milk
- 1/4 cup lime juice
- Pinch of salt

Instructions:

1. In a blender, combine avocados, heavy cream, condensed milk, lime juice, and salt.
2. Blend until smooth and creamy.
3. Pour into a container and freeze for at least 4 hours.
4. Scoop and serve as a dessert.

Avocado and Tomato Salad

Ingredients:

- 2 ripe avocados, diced
- 1 cup cherry tomatoes, halved
- 1/4 cup diced red onion
- 2 tablespoons olive oil
- 1 tablespoon balsamic vinegar
- Salt and pepper to taste

Instructions:

1. In a bowl, combine avocado, cherry tomatoes, and red onion.
2. Drizzle with olive oil and balsamic vinegar.
3. Season with salt and pepper.
4. Toss gently and serve.

Avocado Pasta

Ingredients:

- 2 ripe avocados
- 1/2 cup fresh basil leaves
- 2 garlic cloves
- 1/4 cup olive oil
- 1 lemon, juiced
- Salt and pepper to taste
- 12 oz pasta of your choice

Instructions:

1. Cook the pasta according to package instructions.
2. In a blender, combine avocados, basil, garlic, olive oil, lemon juice, salt, and pepper. Blend until smooth.
3. Drain the pasta and mix with the avocado sauce.
4. Serve immediately with extra basil and a sprinkle of Parmesan if desired.

Avocado and Cucumber Rolls

Ingredients:

- 1 avocado, sliced
- 1 cucumber, thinly sliced
- 4 large rice paper wraps
- 1/4 cup fresh mint leaves
- 1/4 cup fresh cilantro leaves
- Soy sauce or dipping sauce of choice

Instructions:

1. Soak a rice paper wrap in warm water until soft, then lay it flat on a surface.
2. Place avocado, cucumber, mint, and cilantro in the center.
3. Roll up tightly, folding in the sides as you go.
4. Repeat with remaining ingredients and serve with dipping sauce.

Avocado Deviled Eggs

Ingredients:

- 6 hard-boiled eggs
- 1 avocado
- 1 tablespoon lime juice
- 1/4 teaspoon garlic powder
- Salt and pepper to taste
- Paprika for garnish

Instructions:

1. Cut the eggs in half and remove the yolks.
2. Mash the yolks with the avocado, lime juice, garlic powder, salt, and pepper.
3. Spoon or pipe the mixture back into the egg whites.
4. Garnish with paprika and serve.

Avocado Brownies

Ingredients:

- 1 ripe avocado, mashed
- 1/2 cup coconut oil, melted
- 1 cup sugar
- 2 large eggs
- 1/2 cup cocoa powder
- 1/2 cup almond flour
- 1/4 teaspoon salt
- 1 teaspoon vanilla extract

Instructions:

1. Preheat the oven to 350°F (175°C) and grease a baking dish.
2. In a bowl, mix avocado, coconut oil, sugar, eggs, and vanilla until smooth.
3. Add cocoa powder, almond flour, and salt. Mix until well combined.
4. Pour into the prepared baking dish and bake for 25-30 minutes.
5. Let cool before slicing.

Avocado Chicken Salad

Ingredients:

- 2 cups cooked, shredded chicken
- 1 avocado, diced
- 1/2 cup Greek yogurt
- 1 tablespoon lemon juice
- Salt and pepper to taste
- Optional: chopped celery, red onion, or nuts

Instructions:

1. In a bowl, mix chicken, avocado, Greek yogurt, lemon juice, salt, and pepper.
2. Add optional ingredients if desired.
3. Serve in a sandwich, wrap, or on top of greens.

Avocado and Black Bean Tacos

Ingredients:

- 1 avocado, diced
- 1 can black beans, rinsed and drained
- 1/2 cup diced tomatoes
- 1/4 cup chopped fresh cilantro
- 1 lime, juiced
- 8 small tortillas
- Salt and pepper to taste

Instructions:

1. In a bowl, mix black beans, avocado, tomatoes, cilantro, lime juice, salt, and pepper.
2. Warm the tortillas and fill them with the mixture.
3. Serve with your favorite taco toppings.

Avocado Sushi Rolls

Ingredients:

- 1 cup sushi rice
- 2 tablespoons rice vinegar
- 1 avocado, sliced
- Nori sheets
- Soy sauce for serving

Instructions:

1. Cook sushi rice and mix with rice vinegar.
2. Place a nori sheet shiny side down on a bamboo mat.
3. Spread rice over the nori, leaving a 1-inch border.
4. Place avocado slices on the rice.
5. Roll tightly and slice into pieces.
6. Serve with soy sauce.

Avocado and Mango Salad

Ingredients:

- 1 avocado, diced
- 1 mango, diced
- 1/4 red onion, thinly sliced
- 2 tablespoons fresh lime juice
- Salt and pepper to taste
- Fresh cilantro for garnish

Instructions:

1. In a bowl, mix avocado, mango, red onion, lime juice, salt, and pepper.
2. Garnish with fresh cilantro.
3. Serve as a refreshing side dish.

Avocado and Sweet Potato Toast

Ingredients:

- 1 sweet potato, sliced into 1/4-inch thick slices
- 1 avocado, mashed
- Salt and pepper to taste
- Optional toppings: cherry tomatoes, feta cheese, chili flakes

Instructions:

1. Toast the sweet potato slices until tender.
2. Spread mashed avocado over the sweet potato slices.
3. Season with salt and pepper and add optional toppings.
4. Serve as a healthy snack or breakfast.

Avocado Fries

Ingredients:

- 2 ripe avocados, sliced into wedges
- 1/2 cup flour
- 2 eggs, beaten
- 1 cup breadcrumbs
- Salt and pepper to taste
- Optional: spices like paprika or garlic powder

Instructions:

1. Preheat the oven to 400°F (200°C) and line a baking sheet with parchment paper.
2. Coat avocado wedges in flour, then dip in beaten eggs, and coat with breadcrumbs mixed with salt, pepper, and optional spices.
3. Place on the baking sheet and bake for 20-25 minutes until golden and crispy.
4. Serve with your favorite dipping sauce.

Avocado and Shrimp Salad

Ingredients:

- 1 avocado, diced
- 1/2 pound cooked shrimp
- 1/2 cup cherry tomatoes, halved
- 1/4 cup red onion, diced
- 2 tablespoons fresh lime juice
- Salt and pepper to taste

Instructions:

1. In a bowl, combine avocado, shrimp, cherry tomatoes, red onion, lime juice, salt, and pepper.
2. Mix gently to combine.
3. Serve chilled, garnished with fresh herbs if desired.

Avocado and Feta Toast

Ingredients:

- 1 avocado, mashed
- 2 slices of bread, toasted
- 1/4 cup crumbled feta cheese
- Salt and pepper to taste
- Optional: chili flakes or lemon zest

Instructions:

1. Spread mashed avocado over the toasted bread.
2. Sprinkle with crumbled feta cheese.
3. Season with salt, pepper, and optional toppings.
4. Serve immediately.

Avocado Chocolate Mousse

Ingredients:

- 2 ripe avocados
- 1/2 cup cocoa powder
- 1/2 cup maple syrup or honey
- 1 teaspoon vanilla extract
- Pinch of salt

Instructions:

1. In a blender, combine avocados, cocoa powder, maple syrup, vanilla extract, and salt.
2. Blend until smooth and creamy.
3. Chill in the refrigerator for at least 1 hour before serving.
4. Serve with whipped cream or fresh berries.

Avocado and Chickpea Salad

Ingredients:

- 1 avocado, diced
- 1 can chickpeas, rinsed and drained
- 1/2 cucumber, diced
- 1/4 cup red onion, diced
- 2 tablespoons lemon juice
- Salt and pepper to taste

Instructions:

1. In a bowl, mix avocado, chickpeas, cucumber, red onion, lemon juice, salt, and pepper.
2. Toss gently to combine.
3. Serve as a refreshing side dish or light meal.

Avocado Pizza

Ingredients:

- 1 pizza crust or flatbread
- 1 avocado, sliced
- 1/2 cup mozzarella cheese
- 1/4 cup cherry tomatoes, halved
- 1 tablespoon olive oil
- Salt and pepper to taste

Instructions:

1. Preheat the oven to 450°F (230°C).
2. Spread mozzarella cheese over the pizza crust.
3. Add avocado slices and cherry tomatoes.
4. Drizzle with olive oil and season with salt and pepper.
5. Bake for 10-12 minutes until the crust is crispy and cheese is melted.
6. Serve hot.

Avocado and Spinach Smoothie

Ingredients:

- 1 avocado
- 1 cup spinach
- 1 banana
- 1 cup almond milk
- 1 tablespoon honey or maple syrup

Instructions:

1. In a blender, combine avocado, spinach, banana, almond milk, and honey or maple syrup.
2. Blend until smooth and creamy.
3. Serve immediately.

Avocado Egg Salad

Ingredients:

- 4 hard-boiled eggs, chopped
- 1 avocado, mashed
- 2 tablespoons mayonnaise
- 1 tablespoon mustard
- Salt and pepper to taste

Instructions:

1. In a bowl, mix chopped eggs, mashed avocado, mayonnaise, mustard, salt, and pepper.
2. Stir until well combined.
3. Serve in a sandwich, wrap, or on top of greens.

Grilled Avocado

Ingredients:

- 2 avocados, halved and pitted
- 1 tablespoon olive oil
- Salt and pepper to taste
- Optional: lime wedges, chili flakes, or fresh herbs

Instructions:

1. Preheat the grill to medium heat.
2. Brush the avocado halves with olive oil and season with salt and pepper.
3. Place avocados on the grill, cut side down, and grill for 4-5 minutes.
4. Remove from the grill and serve with optional toppings.

Avocado and Kale Salad

Ingredients:

- 1 avocado, sliced
- 2 cups kale, chopped
- 1/4 cup almonds, toasted
- 2 tablespoons olive oil
- 1 tablespoon lemon juice
- Salt and pepper to taste

Instructions:

1. In a large bowl, massage kale with olive oil and lemon juice until tender.
2. Add sliced avocado and toasted almonds.
3. Season with salt and pepper.
4. Toss gently and serve.

Avocado and Corn Salad

Ingredients:

- 1 avocado, diced
- 1 cup corn kernels, cooked
- 1/2 red onion, diced
- 1/4 cup fresh cilantro, chopped
- 2 tablespoons lime juice
- Salt and pepper to taste

Instructions:

1. In a bowl, mix avocado, corn, red onion, cilantro, lime juice, salt, and pepper.
2. Toss gently to combine.
3. Serve chilled as a side dish.

Avocado and Lentil Bowl

Ingredients:

- 1 avocado, sliced
- 1 cup cooked lentils
- 1/2 cucumber, diced
- 1/4 cup cherry tomatoes, halved
- 2 tablespoons olive oil
- 1 tablespoon balsamic vinegar
- Salt and pepper to taste

Instructions:

1. In a bowl, combine cooked lentils, cucumber, cherry tomatoes, olive oil, and balsamic vinegar.
2. Top with sliced avocado.
3. Season with salt and pepper.
4. Serve as a hearty meal.

Avocado and Tuna Salad

Ingredients:

- 1 avocado, diced
- 1 can tuna, drained
- 1/4 cup red onion, diced
- 2 tablespoons mayonnaise
- 1 tablespoon lemon juice
- Salt and pepper to taste

Instructions:

1. In a bowl, mix avocado, tuna, red onion, mayonnaise, lemon juice, salt, and pepper.
2. Stir gently until well combined.
3. Serve on toast, crackers, or as a sandwich filling.

Avocado and Beet Salad

Ingredients:

- 1 avocado, sliced
- 2 cooked beets, diced
- 1/4 cup goat cheese, crumbled
- 2 tablespoons olive oil
- 1 tablespoon balsamic vinegar
- Salt and pepper to taste

Instructions:

1. In a bowl, combine beets, olive oil, balsamic vinegar, salt, and pepper.
2. Add sliced avocado and crumbled goat cheese.
3. Toss gently and serve.

Avocado and Edamame Dip

Ingredients:

- 1 avocado, mashed
- 1 cup edamame, shelled and cooked
- 1 tablespoon lime juice
- 1 clove garlic, minced
- Salt and pepper to taste

Instructions:

1. In a blender or food processor, combine mashed avocado, edamame, lime juice, garlic, salt, and pepper.
2. Blend until smooth.
3. Serve with chips or vegetables.

Avocado and Roasted Vegetable Sandwich

Ingredients:

- 1 avocado, sliced
- 1 cup assorted roasted vegetables (zucchini, bell peppers, eggplant)
- 2 slices of bread or a baguette
- 2 tablespoons hummus or mayonnaise

Instructions:

1. Spread hummus or mayonnaise on the bread.
2. Layer roasted vegetables and avocado slices.
3. Assemble the sandwich and serve.

Avocado and Bacon Salad

Ingredients:

- 1 avocado, diced
- 4 slices of bacon, cooked and crumbled
- 2 cups mixed greens
- 1/4 cup cherry tomatoes, halved
- 2 tablespoons olive oil
- 1 tablespoon red wine vinegar
- Salt and pepper to taste

Instructions:

1. In a large bowl, combine mixed greens, avocado, cherry tomatoes, and crumbled bacon.
2. Drizzle with olive oil and red wine vinegar.
3. Season with salt and pepper.
4. Toss gently and serve.

Avocado and Crab Salad

Ingredients:

- 1 avocado, diced
- 1/2 cup cooked crab meat
- 1/4 cup cucumber, diced
- 2 tablespoons mayonnaise
- 1 tablespoon lemon juice
- Salt and pepper to taste

Instructions:

1. In a bowl, mix avocado, crab meat, cucumber, mayonnaise, lemon juice, salt, and pepper.
2. Stir gently to combine.
3. Serve on lettuce leaves or as a sandwich filling.

Avocado and Pesto Pasta

Ingredients:

- 1 avocado, mashed
- 1/2 cup basil pesto
- 8 oz pasta of your choice
- 1/4 cup cherry tomatoes, halved
- 2 tablespoons olive oil
- Salt and pepper to taste

Instructions:

1. Cook pasta according to package instructions. Drain and set aside.
2. In a bowl, mix mashed avocado and pesto.
3. Toss the pasta with the avocado pesto mixture.
4. Add cherry tomatoes and drizzle with olive oil.
5. Season with salt and pepper, then serve.

Avocado and Watermelon Salad

Ingredients:

- 1 avocado, diced
- 2 cups watermelon, cubed
- 1/4 cup feta cheese, crumbled
- 2 tablespoons fresh mint, chopped
- 2 tablespoons olive oil
- 1 tablespoon lime juice
- Salt and pepper to taste

Instructions:

1. In a bowl, combine avocado, watermelon, feta cheese, and mint.
2. Drizzle with olive oil and lime juice.
3. Season with salt and pepper.
4. Toss gently and serve chilled.

Avocado and Quinoa Salad

Ingredients:

- 1 avocado, diced
- 1 cup cooked quinoa
- 1/2 cup cucumber, diced
- 1/4 cup red bell pepper, diced
- 2 tablespoons olive oil
- 1 tablespoon lemon juice
- Salt and pepper to taste

Instructions:

1. In a bowl, mix cooked quinoa, cucumber, bell pepper, and avocado.
2. Drizzle with olive oil and lemon juice.
3. Season with salt and pepper.
4. Toss gently and serve.

Avocado and Pineapple Salsa

Ingredients:

- 1 avocado, diced
- 1 cup pineapple, diced
- 1/4 cup red onion, finely chopped
- 1 jalapeño, seeded and diced
- 2 tablespoons fresh cilantro, chopped
- 1 tablespoon lime juice
- Salt to taste

Instructions:

1. In a bowl, combine avocado, pineapple, red onion, jalapeño, and cilantro.
2. Drizzle with lime juice and season with salt.
3. Toss gently and serve as a dip or topping.

Avocado and Cucumber Soup

Ingredients:

- 1 avocado, peeled and pitted
- 1 cucumber, peeled and chopped
- 1 cup vegetable broth
- 2 tablespoons lime juice
- Salt and pepper to taste
- Fresh dill for garnish

Instructions:

1. In a blender, combine avocado, cucumber, vegetable broth, lime juice, salt, and pepper.
2. Blend until smooth.
3. Chill in the refrigerator for 1-2 hours.
4. Garnish with fresh dill before serving.

Avocado and Zucchini Noodles

Ingredients:

- 1 avocado, mashed
- 2 zucchinis, spiralized
- 1/4 cup cherry tomatoes, halved
- 2 tablespoons olive oil
- 1 tablespoon lemon juice
- Salt and pepper to taste

Instructions:

1. In a bowl, mix mashed avocado, olive oil, and lemon juice.
2. Toss zucchini noodles with the avocado mixture.
3. Add cherry tomatoes and season with salt and pepper.
4. Serve immediately.

Avocado and Pea Smash

Ingredients:

- 1 avocado, mashed
- 1 cup green peas, cooked
- 1 tablespoon lemon juice
- 1 clove garlic, minced
- Salt and pepper to taste

Instructions:

1. In a bowl, combine mashed avocado, cooked peas, lemon juice, and garlic.
2. Mash until well combined.
3. Season with salt and pepper.
4. Serve on toast or as a dip.

Avocado and Radish Salad

Ingredients:

- 1 avocado, diced
- 1/2 cup radishes, thinly sliced
- 1/4 cup arugula
- 2 tablespoons olive oil
- 1 tablespoon balsamic vinegar
- Salt and pepper to taste

Instructions:

1. In a bowl, mix avocado, radishes, and arugula.
2. Drizzle with olive oil and balsamic vinegar.
3. Season with salt and pepper.
4. Toss gently and serve.

Avocado and Smoked Salmon Salad

Ingredients:

- 1 avocado, diced
- 4 oz smoked salmon, torn into pieces
- 2 cups mixed greens (arugula, spinach, etc.)
- 1/4 red onion, thinly sliced
- 1 tablespoon olive oil
- 1 tablespoon lemon juice
- Salt and pepper to taste

Instructions:

1. In a large bowl, combine the mixed greens, avocado, smoked salmon, and red onion.
2. Drizzle with olive oil and lemon juice.
3. Season with salt and pepper to taste.
4. Toss gently and serve.

Avocado and Eggplant Spread

Ingredients:

- 1 avocado, peeled and pitted
- 1 small eggplant, roasted and mashed
- 1 tablespoon tahini
- 1 clove garlic, minced
- 1 tablespoon lemon juice
- Salt and pepper to taste

Instructions:

1. Roast the eggplant until soft and mash it with a fork.
2. In a bowl, combine the mashed eggplant, avocado, tahini, garlic, and lemon juice.
3. Season with salt and pepper and mix until smooth.
4. Serve as a spread with pita or crackers.

Avocado and Roasted Pepper Salad

Ingredients:

- 1 avocado, diced
- 1 roasted red bell pepper, chopped
- 1 cup cherry tomatoes, halved
- 2 tablespoons olive oil
- 1 tablespoon balsamic vinegar
- Salt and pepper to taste

Instructions:

1. In a bowl, combine the avocado, roasted red pepper, and cherry tomatoes.
2. Drizzle with olive oil and balsamic vinegar.
3. Season with salt and pepper to taste.
4. Toss gently and serve.

Avocado and Arugula Salad

Ingredients:

- 1 avocado, diced
- 2 cups arugula
- 1/4 cup cucumber, thinly sliced
- 1 tablespoon olive oil
- 1 tablespoon lemon juice
- Salt and pepper to taste

Instructions:

1. In a bowl, toss arugula, avocado, and cucumber together.
2. Drizzle with olive oil and lemon juice.
3. Season with salt and pepper to taste.
4. Toss gently and serve immediately.

Avocado and Lime Sorbet

Ingredients:

- 2 ripe avocados, peeled and pitted
- 1/2 cup lime juice
- 1/2 cup coconut water
- 1/4 cup honey or agave syrup (optional)

Instructions:

1. In a blender, combine avocado, lime juice, coconut water, and honey/agave syrup.
2. Blend until smooth and creamy.
3. Pour the mixture into a shallow dish and freeze for at least 4 hours, stirring occasionally.
4. Once frozen, scoop and serve as sorbet.

Avocado and Roasted Chickpea Bowl

Ingredients:

- 1 avocado, diced
- 1 cup roasted chickpeas (store-bought or homemade)
- 1/2 cup quinoa, cooked
- 1/4 cup cucumber, diced
- 1 tablespoon olive oil
- 1 tablespoon lemon juice
- Salt and pepper to taste

Instructions:

1. In a bowl, layer quinoa, roasted chickpeas, cucumber, and avocado.
2. Drizzle with olive oil and lemon juice.
3. Season with salt and pepper to taste.
4. Toss gently and serve as a nutritious bowl.